101

Featuring Ukulele Tablature, Play-Along Tracks, History, and Much More!

UKULELE LICKS

Essential Blues, Jazz, Country, Bluegrass, and Rock 'n' Roll Licks for the Uke

By Lil' Rev

ISBN 978-1-4234-8264-2

HAL•LEONARD CORPORATION
7777 W. BLUEMOUND RD. P.O. BOX 13819 MILWAUKEE, WI 53213

T0116702

In Australia Contact:
Hal Leonard Australia Pty. Ltd.
4 Lentara Court
Cheltenham, Victoria, 3192 Australia
Email: ausadmin@halleonard.com.au

Visit Hal Leonard Online at
www.halleonard.com

Introduction

Hello, and welcome to *101 Licks for Ukulele*. This unique collection of blues, jazzy blues, country, bluegrass, and rock 'n' roll licks should supply you with a lifetime of great ideas which you can use to flavor your favorite tunes.

Since the beginning of recorded sounds, musicians from every genre have spent countless hours studying the recorded works of their favorite artists in order to master signature riffs, and, in doing so, gain command of a given style. It is never enough to run scales and play exercises all day in order to develop your own sound. If you truly want to be a stylistic player, it is essential that you learn to cop licks from the great masters. In listening to legendary players like Lonnie Johnson, T-Bone Walker, Buddy Guy, Stevie Ray Vaughan, and so many others, you will soon begin to hear the evolution of these classic riffs unfold before your very ears as they are passed from one generation to the next. It is my sincere hope that as you begin to master these wonderful, little nuggets of musical soul, you will be inspired to seek out the recorded works of the artists featured in these pages.

While a great many of these riffs can trace their origins to instruments other than the ukulele, they all have one thing in common: they were chosen because they work particularly well on our humble, little box of joy—the ukulele. Today, the ukulele world is witnessing a flowering of instrumental prowess—the likes of which we have never before seen! As this revival begins to unfold, and we all become more familiar with signature licks from the growing legion of masterful players, the reservoir of ukulele riffs that players draw from will continue to grow!

To get the most out of this book, I encourage you to jump around, and learn a lick or two in each key and section. This will give you a good overview of the different genres and styles while also helping to build your arsenal of licks over a broad range of keys and time signatures. Eventually, some of these licks will become your favorites; others may only be used once in a while. As you go along, be sure to note each section's recommended listening, and typical scale and chord progression, as they will help familiarize you with how these riffs work with various chords and their respective scales.

Enjoy, and happy picking!

– Lil' Rev

Musical Symbols

Music is written with notes on a **staff**. The staff has five lines and four spaces between the lines. Where a note is written on the staff determines its pitch (highness or lowness). At the beginning of the staff is a clef sign. Ukulele music is written in the treble clef.

Each line and space of the staff has a letter name. The **lines** are (from bottom to top) E–G–B–D–F, which you can remember as "Every Good Boy Does Fine." The **spaces** are (from bottom to top) F–A–C–E, which spells "face."

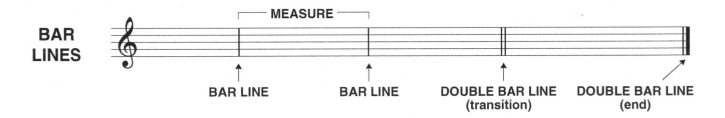

The staff is divided into several parts by bar lines. The space between two bar lines is called a **measure** (also known as a "bar"). At the end of a piece of music a double bar is placed on the staff.

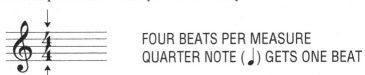

Each measure contains a group of **beats**. Beats are the steady pulse of music. You respond to the pulse or beat when you tap your foot.

The two numbers place next to the clef sign are the **time signature**. The top number tells you how many beats are in one measure

FOUR BEATS PER MEASURE
QUARTER NOTE (♩) GETS ONE BEAT

The bottom number of the time signature tells you what kind of note will receive one beat.

Notes indicate the length (number of counts) of a musical sound.

NOTE VALUES

WHOLE NOTE = 4 beats   HALF NOTE = 2 beats   QUARTER NOTE = 1 beat

When different kinds of notes are placed on different lines or spaces, you will know the pitch of the note and how long to play the sound.

Ukulele Notation Legend

THE MUSICAL STAFF shows pitches and rhythms and is divided by bar lines into measures. Pitches are named after the first seven letters of the alphabet.

TABLATURE graphically represents the ukulele fingerboard. Each horizontal line represents a a string, and each number represents a fret.

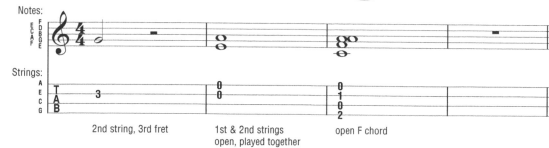

2nd string, 3rd fret

1st & 2nd strings open, played together

open F chord

HALF-STEP BEND: Strike the note and bend up 1/2 step.

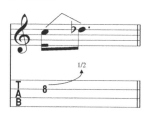

WHOLE-STEP BEND: Strike the note and bend up one step.

GRACE NOTE BEND: Strike the note and immediately bend up as indicated.

SLIGHT (MICROTONE) BEND: Strike the note and bend up 1/4 step.

BEND AND RELEASE: Strike the note and bend up as indicated, then release back to the original note. Only the first note is struck.

PRE-BEND: Bend the note as indicated, then strike it.

VIBRATO: The string is vibrated by rapidly bending and releasing the note with the fretting hand.

HAMMER-ON: Strike the first (lower) note with one finger, then sound the higher note (on the same string) with another finger by fretting it without picking.

PULL-OFF: Place both fingers on the notes to be sounded. Strike the first note and without picking, pull the finger off to sound the second (lower) note.

LEGATO SLIDE: Strike the first note and then slide the same fret-hand finger up or down to the second note. The second note is not struck.

SHIFT SLIDE: Same as legato slide, except the second note is struck.

TRILL: Very rapidly alternate between the notes indicated by continuously hammering on and pulling off.

TREMOLO PICKING: The note is picked as rapidly and continuously as possible.

Additional Musical Definitions

 (accent)
- Accentuate note (play it louder)

 (staccato)
- Play the note short

D.S. al Coda
- Go back to the sign (%), then play until the measure marked "*To Coda*," then skip to the section labelled "**Coda**."

D.C. al Fine
- Go back to the beginning of the song and play until the measure marked "*Fine*" (end).

N.C.
- No chord.

- Repeat measures between signs.

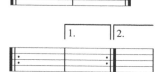
- When a repeated section has different endings, play the first ending only the first time and the second ending only the second time.

NOTE: Tablature numbers in parentheses mean:

1. The note is being sustained over a system (note in standard notation is tied), or

2. The note is sustained, but a new articulation (such as a hammer-on, pull-off, slide or vibrato) begins, or

3. The note is a barely audible "ghost" note (note in standard notation is also in parentheses).

The 101 Licks Scale Finder

Use this handy page as a reference guide for your study of how licks relate to various keys and scales. While most of the licks in this book lean heavily on the major and minor pentatonic scales, you should also familiarize yourself with some of the other modes and scales displayed here. The following scales are all transposable to any key by simply moving the root note to the intended note.

The *Hal Leonard Ukulele Scale Finder* might also be valuable to a student who is looking to complement their mastery of these licks with a thorough understanding of scale theory—up and down the neck. Good luck and happy picking!

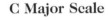 = root note ◯ = open string

C Major Scale
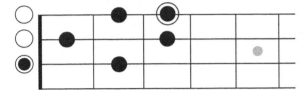

C Major Scale – Pattern 2
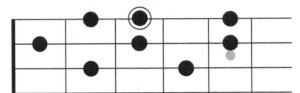

C Blues Scale
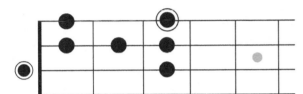

C Blues Scale – Pattern 2
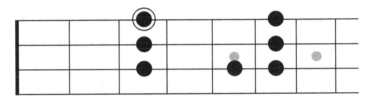

C Minor Pentatonic Scale

C Minor Pentatonic Scale – Pattern 2

C Major Pentatonic Scale

C Major Pentatonic Scale – Pattern 2

C Composite Blues Scale
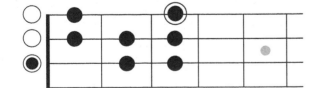

C Composite Blues Scale – Pattern 2
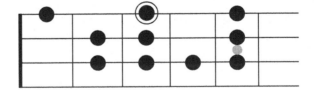

C Mixolydian Mode
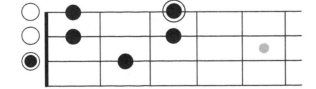

C Dorian Mode
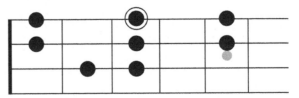

Blues Licks in A

Lonnie Johnson, Eddie Lang, and Charlie Christian—all of these legends have peppered their playing with blues-based riffs, yet none left as vast a library of licks as the great T-Bone Walker. While his playing was expressive, it was often understated and highly adaptable to the ukulele. This first lick is moveable, so try it out up and down the neck. This works well over the I chord in A—especially when played as an A9, A6, or A7.

Track 1
(0:00)

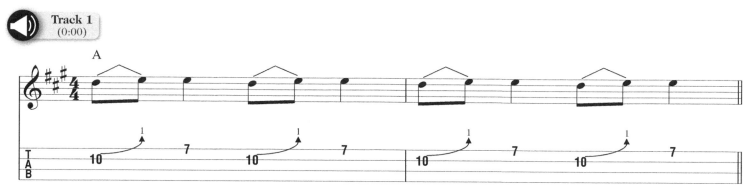

Here is another lick to be played over the I chord (A). This is classic T-Bone all the way. Again, I encourage you to move these up and down the neck.

Track 1
(0:09)

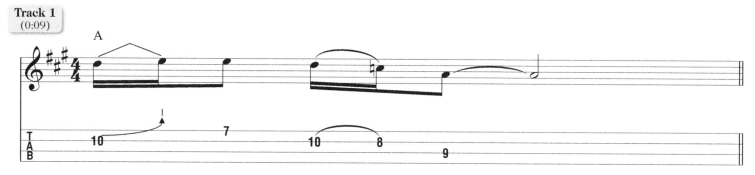

Single-line playing in today's ukulele world is also filled with riff-based phrasing from Lyle Ritz and Bill Tapia to James Hill (and yours truly). Here is a T-Bone-like lick that I have heard almost everybody play! Whether they knew it to be a T-Bone-inspired phrase is not as important as the fact that it has become an unconscious part of the American single-string lead vocabulary. You can also use this over the IV chord (D9) in a jazzy blues.

Track 1
(0:17)

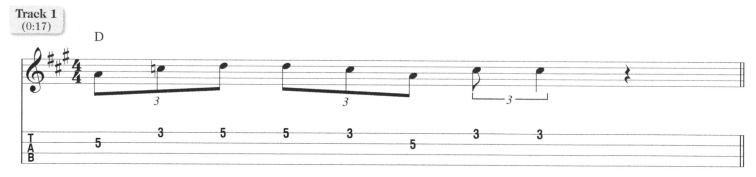

Dig this basic Blues riff á la Robert Johnson. Use this lick over the I chord in A.

Track 1
(0:24)

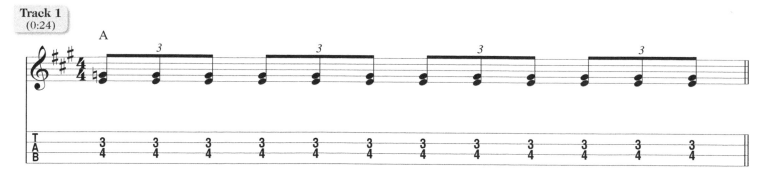

More Blues Licks in A

The following lick creates an eerie blues effect that is seldom heard on ukulele. To do it, slide the F♯ up one half step to G natural, and you'll be riding high like Stevie Ray Vaughan! Imagine if Stevie had been a uke player! This riff works best over the I chord in A, and is especially useful when played against a ninth chord.

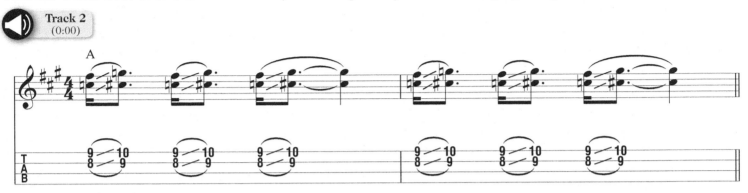

Here is another generic, down-home lick from the late 1940s when Delta bluesmen left the rural south and moved north to Chicago. This works well over the V chord (E) in A.

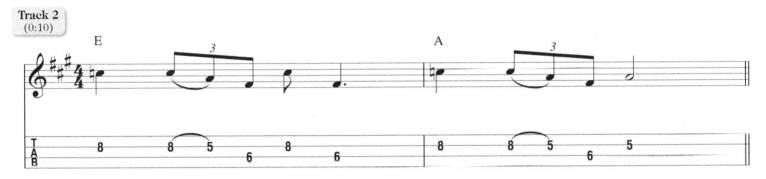

Solid licks needn't be a blistering barrage of notes. Remember: less is more—especially with ukulele. This lick works well over the V chord (E) in A. It is in the spirit of Jimmy Rogers, who was Muddy Waters' band mate.

The final lick in A is about as classic as they come—from Howlin' Wolf and Carl Perkins to Scotty Moore and the Allman Brothers. This lick is pure American history, and it can be used as either an intro or a turnaround in A.

Blues Chords & Scales in A

Typical A Blues Chord Progression

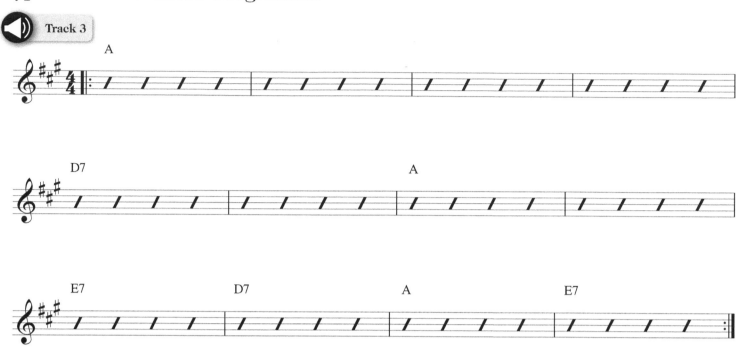

Track 3

Note: When practicing these typical chord progressions, it is advisable that you also experiment playing these patterns with both sixth and ninth chords so you can begin to hear how the licks relate to other commonly-used chord voicings.

Scales Often Used

- A Major Pentatonic
- A Minor Pentatonic
- A Blues
- A Mixolydian

Recommended Listening

Artist	Album/Song Title
T-Bone Walker	*The Imperial Recordings (1950–1954)*
Eddie Lang	*The New York Sessions (1926–1935)*
Bill Tapia	*Living It Live*
Lonnie Johnson	*Classics (1948–49)*
Buddy Guy	*As Good as It Gets*
Little Milton	*Grits Ain't Groceries*
Stevie Ray Vaughan	*The Greatest Hits Volume 2*
Howlin' Wolf	*Killing Floor*

Blues Licks in B♭

By and large, a great deal of blues playing relies heavily on the triplet feel for its rhythmic nuance. So, here is a minor pentatonic-based lick with sixteenth notes to help you switch things up a bit. Albert King, while not quite as jazzy, leans on a lot of the sixteenth notes for his ferocious sound.

Here's a jazzy blues lick that works well over the I chord (B♭) á la Lyle Ritz.

The following lick is a classic T-Bone Walker-ism. While we learned this same lick in the key of A, let this serve as a reminder that many of these licks can be moved up and down the neck, as well as to other keys. My hope is that you will experiment with them to expand your grab bag of riffs. This works best over a B♭9 chord, or the I chord in B♭.

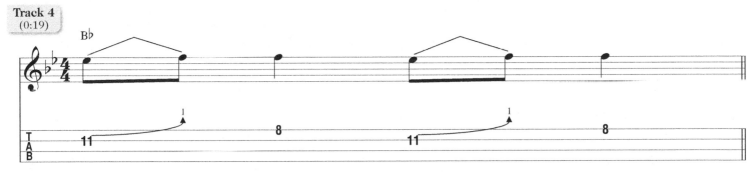

Here's a great one-bar lick that can be played over the V chord (F) in any B♭ progression. Try it against an F9 shape, and see how it really sings!

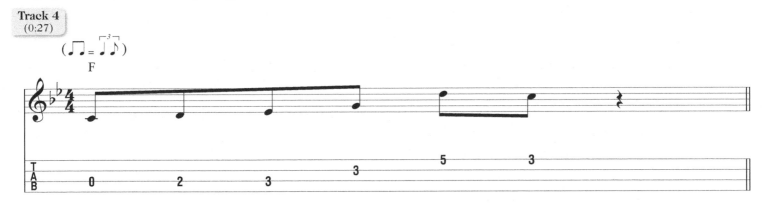

Boogie Riffs in B♭

Single-string blues playing doesn't get much better than the boogie woogie. The following four licks can be used in a solo or as accompaniment. Play this over the I chord (B♭).

Track 5 (0:00)

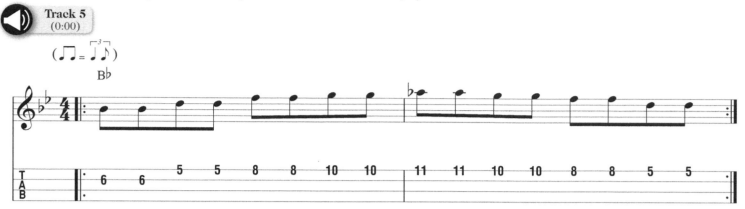

Play this over the IV chord (E♭) change in measures five and six of a 12-bar progression in B♭.

Track 5 (0:11)

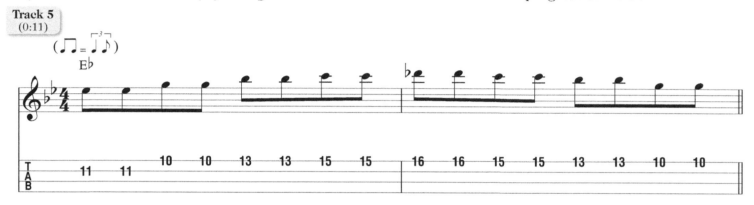

Repeat the first lick (at the top of the page) for two measures, then play the following over the V chord in measure nine of a 12-bar blues in B♭.

Track 5 (0:19)

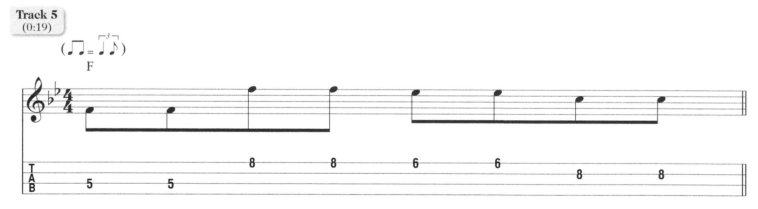

Lastly, this would be played over measure ten of a 12-bar blues in B♭.

Track 5 (0:25)

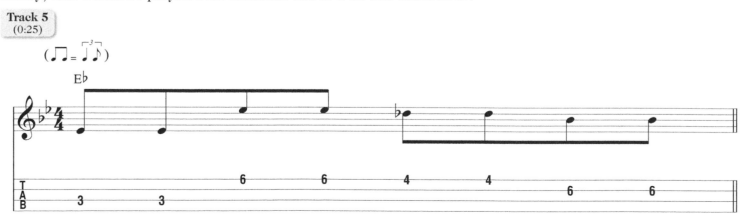

Blues Chords & Scales in B♭

Typical B♭ Blues Chord Progression

 Track 6

B♭7

E♭7   B♭7

F7   E♭7   B♭7   G♭7   F7

Scales Often Used

- B♭ Major Pentatonic
- B♭ Minor Pentatonic
- B♭ Blues
- B♭ Mixolydian

Recommended Listening

Artist	Album/Song Title
Albert King	*Stax Profiles*
Lyle Ritz	*How About Uke?*
T-Bone Walker	*The Complete Mosaic Recordings*
Johnny Moore	*This One Time Baby*
Floyd Dixon	*The Complete Aladdin Recordings*
Bessie Smith	*Roots 'N' Blues/Columbia*

Blues Licks in C

This one is short but sweet, and employs slides, pull-offs, vibrato, and hammer-on techniques to great effect. This is just the sort of lick that would be played by Buddy Guy or Eric Clapton, and works best over a V chord (G) in a C blues.

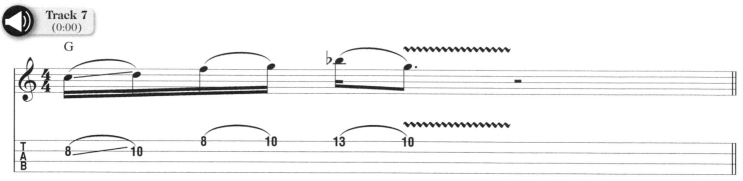

Unleash the rock 'n' roller in you with this next lick; it uses standard, Chuck Berry-like bends throughout. This plays well over the V chord (G) in a C blues.

While ukulele players may be familiar with the triplet stroke, most budding soloists still need to develop a good feel for triplet-based phrasing, as in the following, á la Freddie King. This plays well off the C, F, or G chords in a C blues progression.

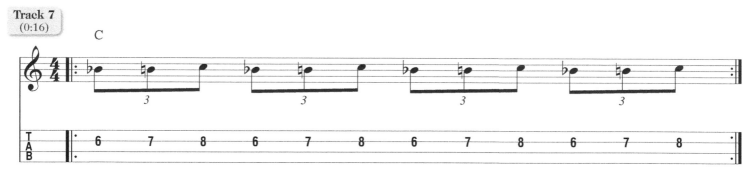

This classy, single-note turnaround comes from the playing of Lonnie Johnson.

More Blues Licks in C

Next time someone says that you can't play blues on the ukulele, play them this classic Buddy Guy-influenced, Chicago-blues-based lick.

Track 8
(0:00)

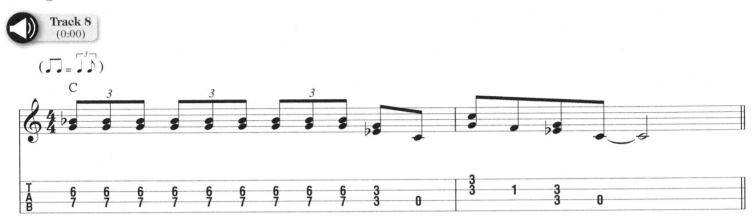

Here is a simple lick that you can play over the V chord (G) in the key of C. Remember: less is more with the blues!

Track 8
(0:10)

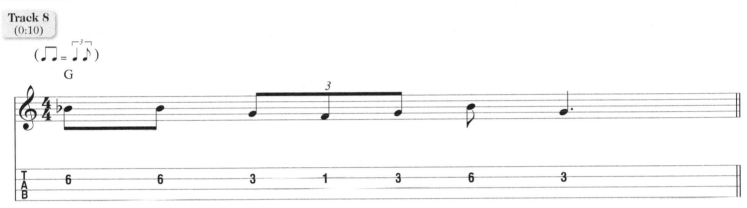

Texas blues is notorious for being low down, gut wrenching, and groovy—all at once. Here is one in the spirit of my personal hero, Johnny "Clyde" Copeland.

Track 8
(0:17)

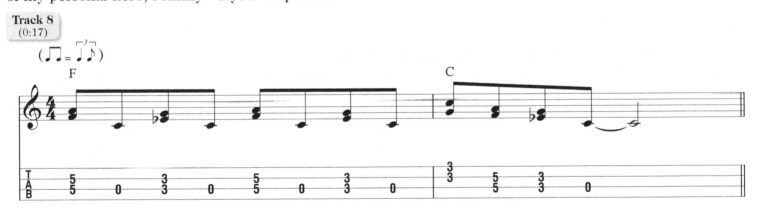

Try this tasty little lick (á la Lil' Rev) over the V chord in C.

Track 8
(0:27)

Blues Chords & Scales in C

Typical C Blues Chord Progression

 Track 9

Scales Often Used

- C Major Pentatonic
- C Minor Pentatonic
- C Blues

Recommended Listening	
Artist	**Album/Song Title**
Johnny "Clyde" Copeland	*Texas Twister*
Buddy Guy	*The Complete Vanguard Recordings*
Eric Clapton	*Backless*
James Hill	*True Love Don't Weep*
Lil' Rev	*Drop Baby Drop*
Chuck Berry	*The Complete Chess Recordings*
Lonnie Johnson	*The Essential Lonnie Johnson*
Freddie King	*Texas Cannonball*

Blues Licks in D

Let's start off with a very cool, down-home, Delta-style lick, much like you'd hear Muddy Waters play on the guitar. Play this over the D chord.

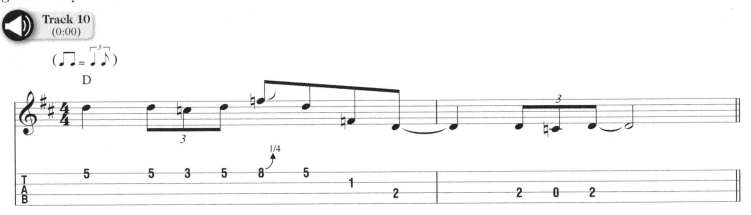

This is a standard lick that I often play in the spirit of Magic Sam. This lick can be played over the IV chord (G) in D.

Next to T-Bone Walker, B.B. King is my all-time favorite source for single-string lead work. Here is a nice lick in D that you can use over the IV (G) chord.

Here's another cool lick á la B.B. King over the V chord (A) in D.

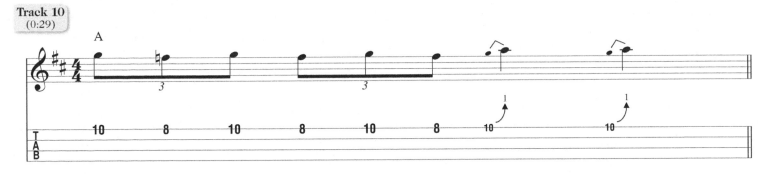

More Blues Licks in D

The old blues guys used to love to play in first position in order to utilize the open strings as much as possible. Play this over the I (D) chord.

Here is a simple little lick to play over the V (A) in D. Watch the slide from F♯ to G.

Track 11 (0:10)

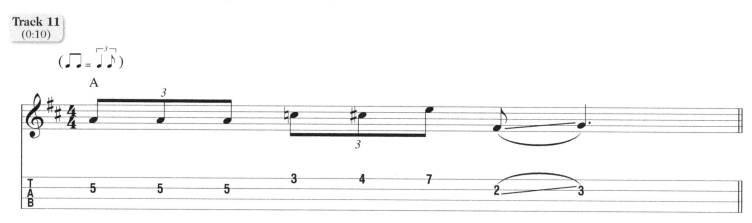

This next lick could prove to be useful not only as a blues lick, but as a rock or country lick as well. Use this over any of the I, IV, or V chords (D, G, or A).

Track 11 (0:18)

This last lick grew out of the boogie tradition with its single-string rhythm patterns. Use this over the I chord (D).

Track 11 (0:29)

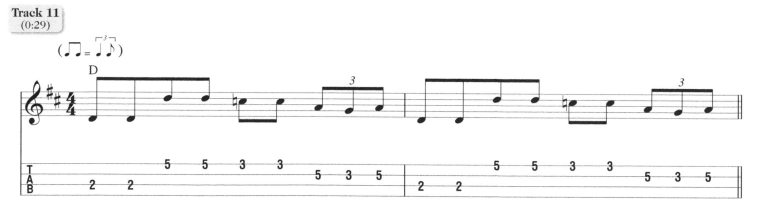

Blues Chords & Scales in D

Typical D Blues Chord Progression

Scales Often Used

- D Major Pentatonic
- D Minor Pentatonic
- D Blues

Recommended Listening

Artist	Album/Song Title
Magic Sam	"Talk to Your Daughter"
Lil' Rev	"Me or Uke Blues"
James Hill	"Obedience Blues"
Jimi Hendrix	"Red House"
Stevie Ray Vaughan	"Love Struck"
Scotty Moore	"Hound Dog"
Muddy Waters	*Folk Singer*
B.B. King	*One Kind Favor*
Magic Slim	"Before You Accuse Me"

Blues Licks in E

This first lick is rooted in the old-time Delta blues tradition, and makes for either a good intro or ending.

This is a classic in the spirit of Muddy Waters.

Here is a cool device that is often employed by jazz and blues players to produce a train whistle effect.

This lick is reminiscent of the late, great bluesman Yank Rachell, who was well known for his mandolin playing (while also being a real, down-home guitarist). This repeating phrase makes a fabulous two- or four-bar intro to a full 12-bar solo.

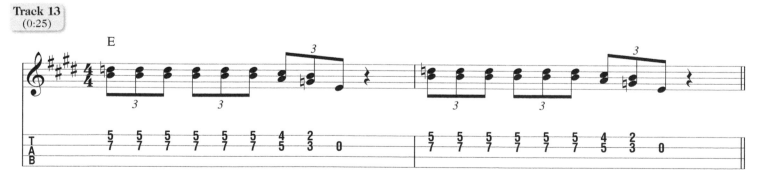

More Blues Licks in E

This next lick is often found in blues/rock circles, and is typical of the repeating motif stock which ends on the root I chord (E). Strike the first note, and slide into the second.

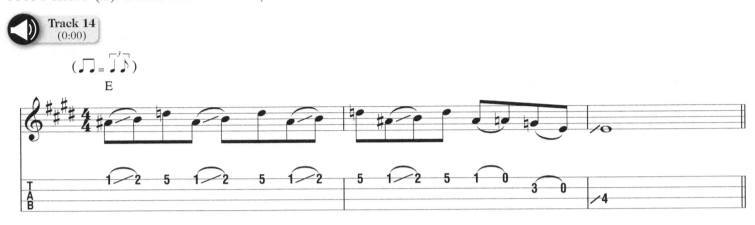

This lick is derived from classic rock phrasing.

This would be used over the V chord (B) in an E blues or rock tune. This is a great riff to practice moving up and down the fretboard.

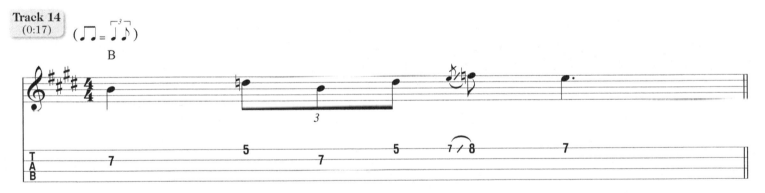

This last lick has been adopted by nearly every Chicago blues-based guitarist today, and is often credited to the late, great Freddie King.

Blues Chords & Scales in E

Typical E Blues Chord Progression

 Track 15

Scales Often Used

- E Major Pentatonic
- E Minor Pentatonic
- E Blues
- E Composite Blues

Recommended Listening	
Artist	**Album/Song Title**
John Lee Hooker	*Boogie Chillen*
ZZ Top	"La Grange"
Lightnin' Hopkins	"Wine Spodee-O-Dee"
Muddy Waters	"Long Distance Call"
Freddie King	"Hideaway"
Lil' Rev	"Dough Won't Rise"
Yank Rachell	"Texas Tony"
Hal Brolund (Manitoba Hal)	*Little Box of Sadness*

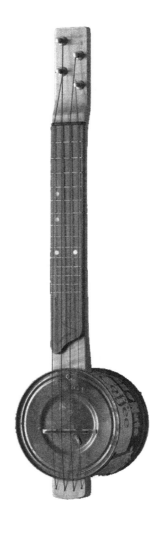

Blues Licks in F

This one is somewhat jazzy, and very tasteful. Use it over the I chord (F) in F.

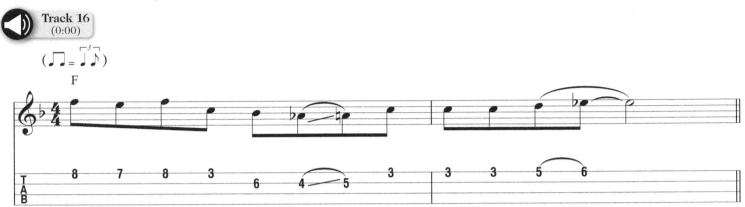

This next lick in F is also a little jazzy, and is reminiscent of the sort of licks that Bill Tapia might play over a Duke Ellington tune.

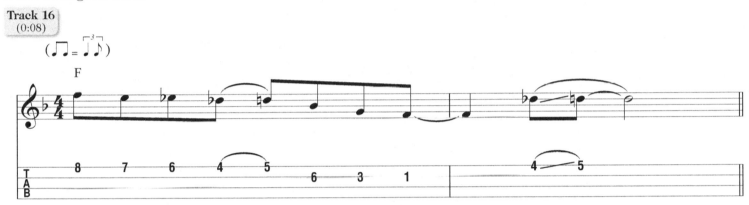

This lick has a great, swinging-eighth feel, and sounds fabulous when played over an F7 chord shape. It is just the sort of curious little lick that might emanate from the strings of surf king Dick Dale.

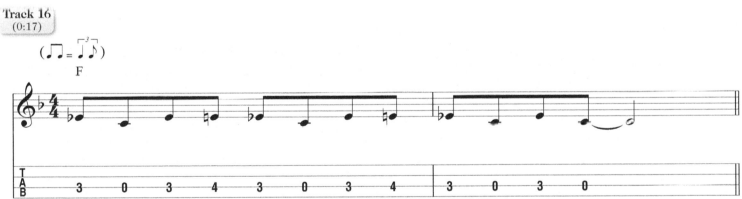

Here's one that has a blues/rock-based feel. Use it against an F chord.

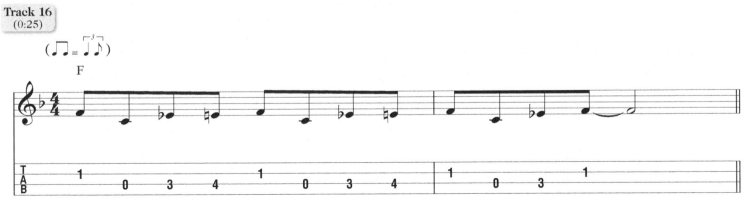

More Blues Licks in F

The lick below utilizes a full-step bend from B♭ up to C. This takes you through classic blues evolution from T-Bone Walker to Chuck Berry, and on to Jimi Hendrix. Use this lick over an F (V) chord in B♭.

Track 17
(0:00)

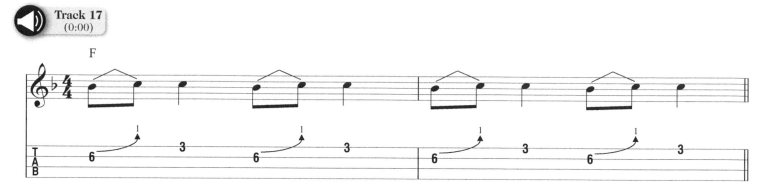

Here's a jazzy blues lick that leans on the F blues scale for its haunting effect. Use it over the F chord. It makes a nice ending, too.

Track 17
(0:10)

This next lick works great over the IV chord (B♭) in F when jamming on a 12-bar blues in F.

Track 17
(0:19)

This last phrase will take you through a classic V–IV (C–B♭) chord change as you move through a 12-bar in F.

Track 17
(0:28)

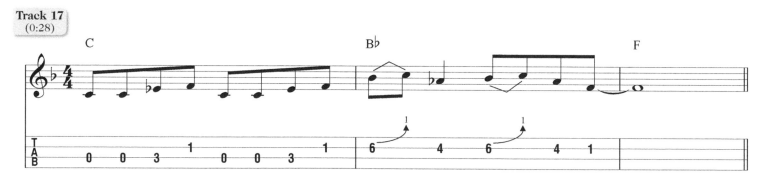

Blues Chords & Scales in F

Typical F Blues Chord Progression

 Track 18

Scales Often Used

- F Major Pentatonic
- F Minor Pentatonic
- F Blues
- F Composite Blues

Recommended Listening

Artist	Album/Song Title
Robert Johnson	*The Complete Recordings*
Muddy Waters	*The Chess Box*
Magic Sam	*West Side Soul*
Buddy Guy	*Buddy Guy*
Howlin' Wolf	*The Chess Box*
Dick Dale	*King of the Surf Guitar*
Jake Shimabukuro	"While My Guitar Gently Weeps"
Roy Smeck	"Nifty Pickin'"
Jimmie Rodgers	"Tuck Away My Lonesome Blues"
Lyle Ritz	"Ritz Cracker"

The Golden Years of the Ukulele (1920s & 1930s)

The "jumping flea" (as the ukulele is often called) has followed a curious, if not humble, path towards greatness, beginning first in 1879, when the *SS Ravenscrag* sailed from Madeira, Portugal, to Hawaii, bringing with it over four hundred Portuguese men, women, and children. While most came to work on sugar plantations, a good many of these workers were skilled in other trades such as cabinet making, cask making, and instrument building. Among these craftsmen were Augusto Dias, Manuel Nunes, and Jose do Espirito Santo—the three men who would give birth to the ukulele industry.

By 1915, the Panama-Pacific International Exposition would seal the ukulele's fate on the mainland, as it was prominently featured at the Hawaii Pavilion, and during this time, it is said to have been heard by as many as sixteen million people. What transpired shortly after the exposition was nothing less than a full-fledged explosion (ukulelemania) that swept the country. "Hapa-haole" (a song sung in English with a few Hawaiian words thrown in for good measure), "On the Beach at Waikiki," "Tiny Bubbles," "Little Brown Girl," "Little Grass Shack," and "My Honolulu Ukulele Baby" became all the go. It wasn't long before the Hawaiian influence crept into early jazz, blues, and country, as artists from Louis Armstrong to the Yodeling Brakeman, and Jimmie Rodgers all started performing and recording with Hawaiian instrumentation (like steel guitar and ukulele) in the mix.

While the sheet music industry was busy cranking out thousands of songs each year, almost anyone could purchase a Martin, Gibson, Harmony, or Regal ukulele—along with a copy of their favorite tune (with chord symbols to boot). This led to a scourge of Vaudevillian ukulele fanatics. With Vaudeville and Broadway sailing full-steam ahead, a small legion of sensational players emerged and contributed to both the era and the instrument.

One of the greatest virtuoso players of the twenties and thirties was none other than Roy Smeck, who was dubbed "the Wizard of the Strings." Smeck's rendition of "12th Street Rag" was mindboggling in both its rhythmic and melodic intensity. He was notorious for exploiting the little, wooden box's innate potential for novelty humor in that anything musical could possibly come out of the instrument at all! Also rising from the ranks was the era's golden-voiced Cliff Edwards, also known as "Ukulele Ike." Mr. Edwards' smooth vocals and confident strumming led to a series of pop tune songbooks bearing his name, as well as countless 78 records sporting his signature, imitation kazoo singing, which he called "eefin.'" Cliff, along with Wendell Hall, Johnny Marvin, "Ukulele" Bailey, Roy Smeck, and many others helped solidify the ukulele's place in American popular music history.

Blues Licks in G

This first lick is a simple first-string lick that covers a fairly wide range of the fretboard, making it good practice for utilizing all four fingers.

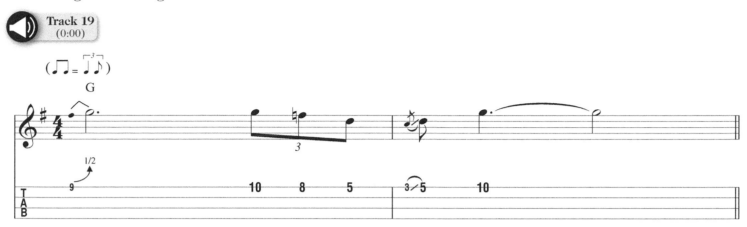

This is a Chicago blues lick á la Jimmy Rodgers (of Muddy Waters fame). Use this over the I chord (G). Really swing it with the triplet feel!

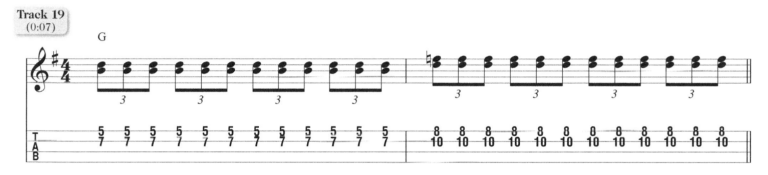

By now, you should be well acquainted with this classic moveable lick á la T-Bone Walker, Chuck Berry, Keith Richards, and Hubert Sumlin (to name a few!). You have already learned to play this in the keys of A and Bb; move it up and down the neck to get the most out of the least. Play this over the I chord in G.

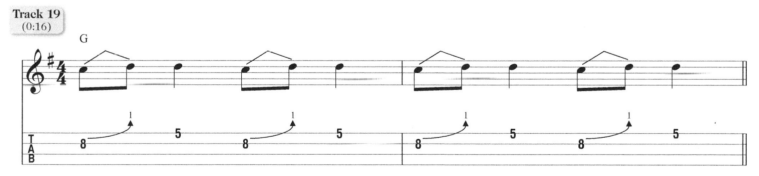

This last lick is a very simple, symmetrical phrase that also works well over the IV chord (C) in a 12-bar blues in G.

The Moveable Blues Lick

This is one of the most valuable licks you can learn! It works well as both an intro to the first measure of a tune, as well as a good lick when used repetitively in a solo. Learn to play it in every key, and it will serve you well as part of your grab bag of licks. Here it is in G.

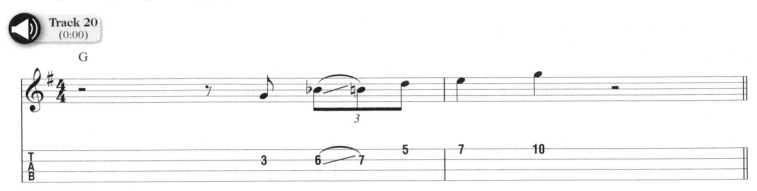

Here is the same lick in the key of F.

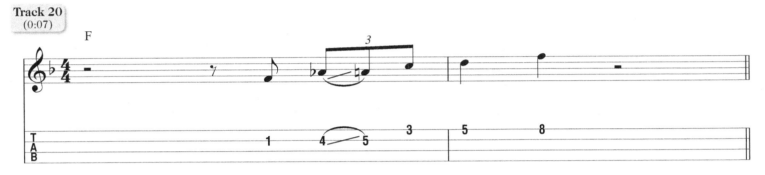

Again, here's the same phrasing, except we're now in the key of A.

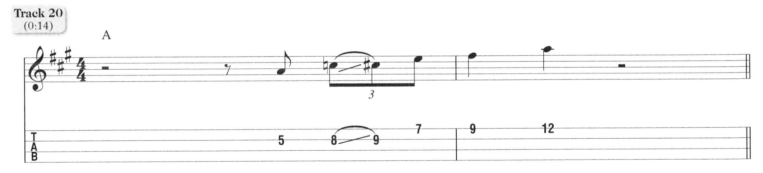

Lastly, moving up the neck a half step from A, try it in the key of Bb.

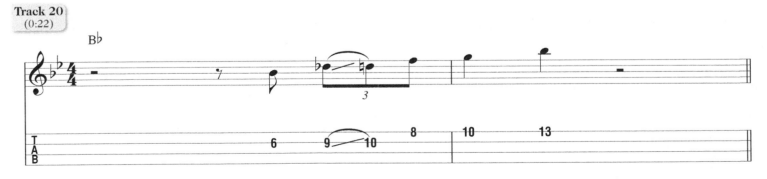

Blues Chords & Scales in G

Typical G Blues Chord Progression

 Track 21

Scales Often Used

- G Major Pentatonic
- G Minor Pentatonic
- G Blues
- G Composite Blues

Recommended Listening	
Artist	**Album/Song Title**
Otis Rush	"So Many Roads, So Many Trains"
Duke Robillard	"T-Bone Shuffle"
T-Bone Walker	*Mean Old World*
Charles Brown	"Tomorrow Night"
Floyd Dixon	"Sad Journey"
Lil' Rev	"St. Louis Blues"
Bill Tapia	"Crazy"
Gerald Ross	"Aboriginal Blue"
Brook Adams	"Purple Haze"

Jazzy Blues Licks

Jazz players like to lean on the blues, and blues players like to lean on jazz to add some spice to their playing. Here is a typical jazzy, blues-based turnaround in the key of C.

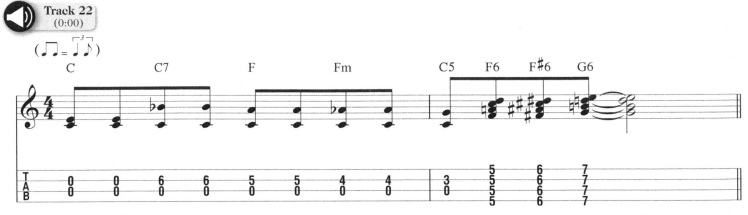

Here, the jazz influence is apparent. Today, licks like this can be heard in the playing of both Bill Tapia and Lyle Ritz. This is a great lick to play over the I chord (B♭9) in any kind of blues or jazz tune.

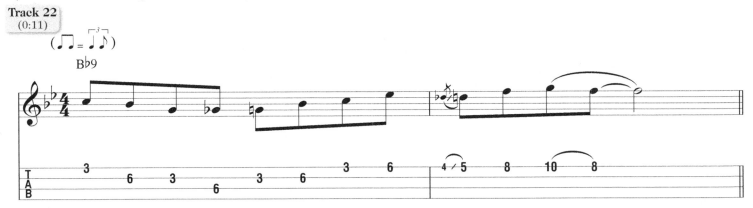

Play this tasty, little lick over the IV chord (B♭7) in F, and really try to swing those eighth notes á la Australian uke star Azo Bell.

This next lick in B♭ sounds good against the root/7th and has a strong jump blues feel to it. Be sure to listen to a lot of Duke Robillard, T-Bone Walker, and Charles Brown for more of these kinds of licks.

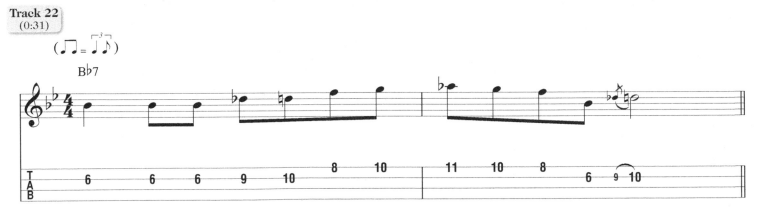

The Moveable Turnaround Lick

As mentioned with regard to the earlier moveable lick in G, the following licks are moveable up and down the neck, making them highly versatile and useful.

Track 23 (0:00)

So far, we've learned this lick in G and F. Now let's try it in A.

Track 23 (0:09)

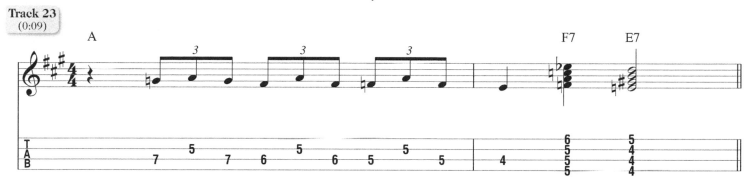

By now, you should be getting a feel for this position as you move it incrementally up or down the neck. Next, we'll try B♭.

Track 23 (0:18)

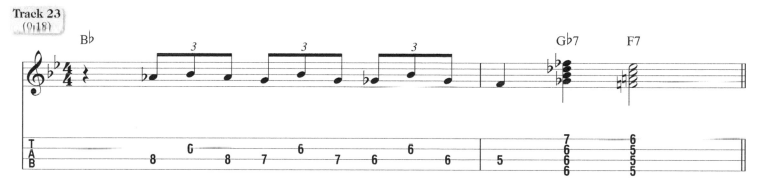

Lastly, let's finish with the people's key of C.

Track 23 (0:27)

Classic Blues Turnaround Licks

This is one of my all-time favorite turnarounds with its boogie-infused feeling and "After Hours" similarity. I would use this with any sort of a jazzy/blues tune.

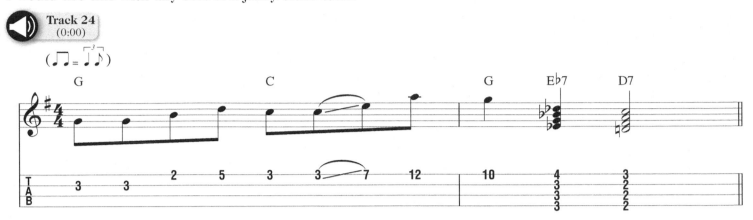

Here's a 1920s-era, descending, double-stop turnaround that works well with any slow blues in F.

The following lick makes for a good intro to a slow-to-medium-paced blues in A.

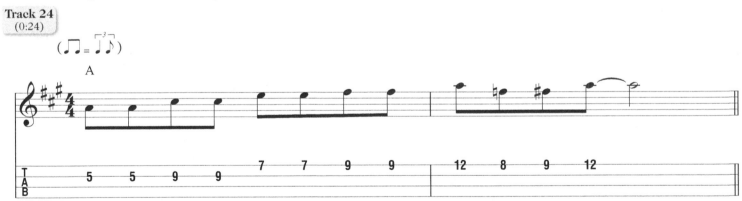

This is a 100% certified Chicago blues turnaround. It is easily moveable up the neck. Use it well!

The Ukulele in Country Music

It wasn't long after the first ukulele appeared on Hawaii's golden shores (in 1879) that it made its way to the mainland, where it took up residence in the hands of hillbilly, blues, and jug band musicians.

Initially, its role was relegated to that of vocal accompaniment and basic rhythm, but as time went on, the humble ukulele began to experience a flowering of talented players who continued to push the perceived limits of the day. Early country bands like the Fiddlin' Powers Family, the Hillbillies, Jimmie Rodgers, Fiddlin' Walter Smith and Friends, Da Costa Woltz's Southern Broadcasters, Ernest V. Stoneman, the Blankenship Family, the Memphis Jug Band, and the Blue Ridge Corn Shuckers used the ukulele to deliver sentimental ballads in both their performance sets and on record. Soon the banjo ukulele took on a role much like that of the mandolin in today's bluegrass. The banjo ukulele created a fascinating rhythm (like a snare drum) for the fiddle to bounce off amidst a backdrop of dance tunes, breakdowns, rags, reels, and waltzes. The most famous performer of the 1920s and 1930s, Jimmie Rodgers (also known as the "Yodeling Brakeman"), thought highly enough of the ukulele's tonality to constantly commit it to wax. Listen to Rodgers' "The Dear Old Sunny South" and "Everybody Does It in Hawaii," as well as other notable country tunes of the day, like the heartfelt "Be Kind to a Man When He's Down," by Price Goodson of Da Costa Woltz's Southern Broadcasters, and "Ukulele" Bob Williams' classic "West Indies Blues."

With ukulele fever going full bore throughout the Vaudeville years, Tin Pan Alley is to thank for fostering a continued sense of interest, as ukulele chords appeared on pop song sheets of the day, and instrument builders like Martin, Gibson, and Regal all worked tirelessly to provide the uke-crazed public with enough ukuleles to put one in almost every household. Non-ukulele-playing hillbilly groups like Charlie Poole and the North Carolina Ramblers often tipped their hats to the ukulele by recording "countrified" versions of the latest sentimental hits like "The Letter That Never Came" and "Budded Roses."

As the ukulele continued its majestic rise to prominence in the roaring 20s, masterful players like Roy Smeck stepped up to display a virtuosity—the likes of which the Vaudeville era had never seen—while Hawaii produced brilliant, melodic players like King Bennie Nawahi and steel guitarist Sol Hoppi. Country music's fascination with all things Hawaiian proliferated throughout the era, and even spilled over into jazz and blues as well.

Today, ukulele players all across America are continuing to put the ukulele to the test in country, bluegrass, western swing, and old-time circles. Check out the work of the Cannote Brothers, Cathy Fink, Lil' Rev, the Barn Kickers, Aaron Keim, Bruce Hutton, Fred Campeau, Brian Hefferan, James Hill, and Linda Higginbotham (with Brad Leftwich), and you too will be amazed that country music is alive and well on the ukulele.

Country Licks in C

Here's a Nashville-style lick á la Danny Gatton. This lick makes for a nice fill, or an even better ending riff.

Track 25
(0:00)

This one is a little spicier! Given its fiddle-tune flavor, play this over any C chord change.

Track 25
(0:08)

And now here's a sweet little C to G lick.

Track 25
(0:16)

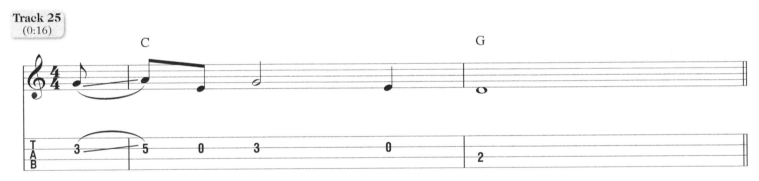

Chicken-picking genius Jerry Reed was fond of these little "chord connector licks."

Track 25
(0:25)

Country Endings in C

This next example is a classic chordal ending in the Nashville vein.

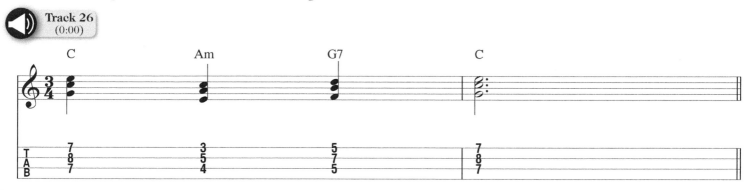

Track 26
(0:00)

Here's a nice lazy country ending in 3/4 time.

Track 26
(0:08)

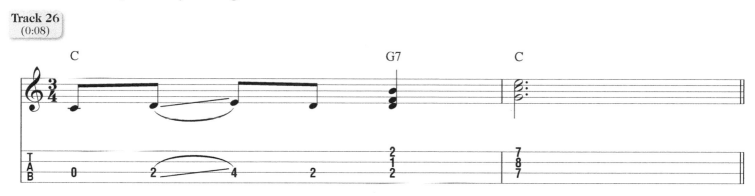

This is a tasty little number, again, in the Nashville tradition.

Track 26
(0:15)

This is an old-school, steel guitar ending. Let it be known that the ukulele and the steel guitar make for a fabulous combination. Try to learn as many of these kinds of licks as possible.

Track 26
(0:22)

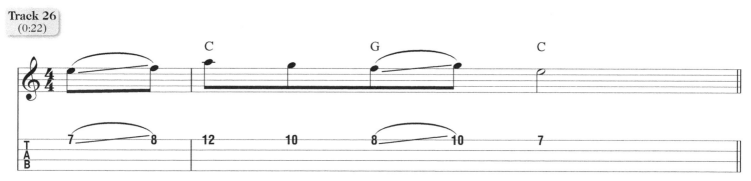

Country Chords & Scales in C

Typical Country Chord Progression in C

 Track 27

Scales Often Used

- C Major
- C Major Pentatonic
- C Mixolydian

Recommended Listening	
Artist	**Album/Song Title**
Johnny Cash	"I Walk the Line"
Marty Robbins	*El Paso*
Lefty Frizzell	"Long Black Veil"
Johnny Horton	"The Battle of New Orleans"
Johnny Horton	"North to Alaska"
Lil' Rev	"When the Wagon Was New"
Pops Bayless	"Flaming Ukulele in the Sky"
The Barnkickers	"Barnkicker Rag"
Norman Blake	"Under the Double Eagle"
The Byrds	*Sweetheart of the Rodeo*

Country Licks in G

Nashville cats like Norman Blake, Tony Rice, and Jerry Douglas often took the standard G run to new heights. Here is where speed and knowing your scales might come in handy… á la James Hill. Play this lick over a G chord.

The roots of country western and western swing deeply intertwine with American fiddle tunes, including reels, waltzes, polkas, and rags. This second lick has a strong fiddle influence to it.

Yes! Even country, like western swing, leans on boogie woogie for some of its influence. Here's one such lick to play over a V chord (D).

Here is a tasty, one-bar lick with a sliding, pedal-steel flavor. Play this over the V chord (D) in G. Look out, Gerald Ross!

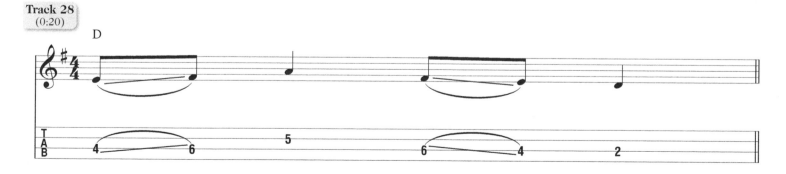

Traditional Country Licks in G

Ukulele players, as I have mentioned, are naturally avid strummers. Below you will find four traditional (early) country licks that can really lift your playing to new heights. You needn't play a full solo to impress the masses. Simply try to connect your chord changes with short fills and runs. Here is a basic D to G lick.

Track 29
(0:00)

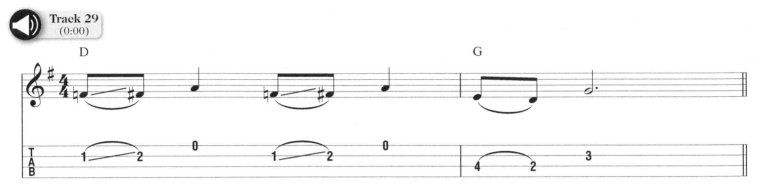

Make a point to learn all of the major and minor pentatonic scales, as well as their respective exercises, and soon you'll be playing lots of licks like this one, played over a stylish V–I (D–G) chord change.

Track 29
(0:09)

Here's a very cool but simple little one-bar G to C lick. These kinds of licks make great little fills between chords, and can really spice up your strumming. I recommend listening to early country guitarists like Riley Puckett and Roy Harvey for similar licks.

Track 29
(0:16)

And here's another one-bar variation from G to C.

Track 29
(0:24)

Note: Now, remember! Many of these licks, like the G to C type, are reciprocal, which means you can play them forward from G to C as written, and then also backwards, from C to G. If you do this, you will get the most use out of these licks.

Country Chords & Scales in G

Typical Country Chord Progression in G

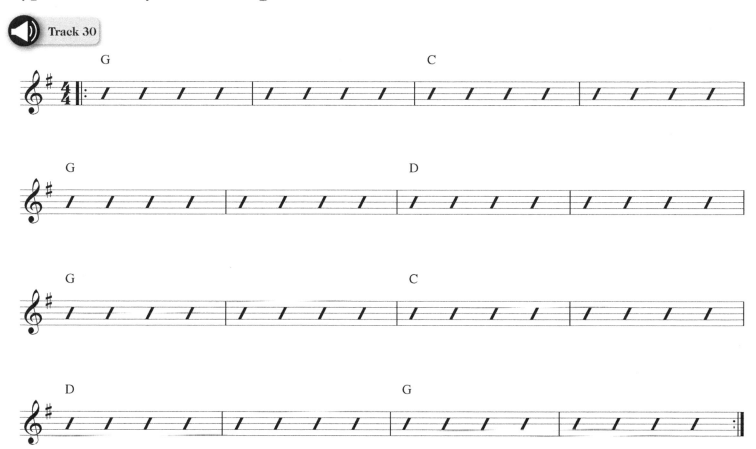

Track 30

Scales Often Used

- G Major
- G Major Pentatonic
- G Major Pentatonic with Flat 3rd
- G Blues

Recommended Listening	
Artist	**Album/Song Title**
Bob Wills & His Texas Playboys	"Brain Cloudy Blues"
Lefty Frizzell	"Always Late (With Your Kisses)"
Johnny Horton	"Honky Tonk Man"
Lil' Rev	"Cripple Creek"
Al Dexter	"Guitar Polka"
Randy Travis	"Forever and Ever, Amen"
Johnny Cash	"Luther Played the Boogie"
Manitoba Hal	"Sixteen Tons"
James Hill	"St. Ann's Reel"

Bluegrass Licks

Playing bluegrass on the ukulele can be highly rewarding, from the swinging eighth notes of fiddle tunes to bluesy embellishments. Stock G-runs and a colorful palette of four-finger riffs will really expand your technical ability to play fast and clean.

This first lick is a typical C to G lick that will help return to the root chord with style and grace (when coming off of the C).

This is also a typical bluegrass motif. This lick is a great exercise in using all four fingers to execute a phrase.

Here is one of my personal favorite ending phrases. Use this lick to end a song—just like you would end with a tag. This is a jaw-dropper in the ukulele world, as it requires speed and finesse to pull off in front of an audience. Practice it well!

This one shows strong ragtime and blues influences employed by many respected bluegrass stalwarts like Tony Rice, Norman Blake, and David Grisman. Use this over any two-bar phrase in D, or repeat it twice and it works well in a 12-bar blues.

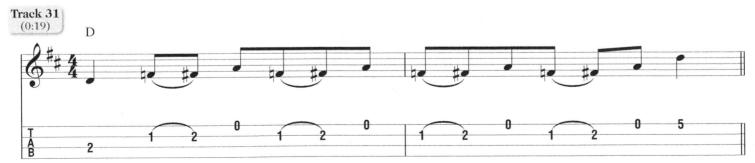

More Bluegrass Licks

Here are a few more standard bluegrass licks for uke. This next lick is a simple phrase you can play over any two bars.

This next lick is similar in feel to the above lick in G, and makes a nice repeating phrase when played over the D chord.

Don't get stuck in the rut of playing everything in a major key! Below is a dandy, little lick to help you get your fingers familiar with the A minor position.

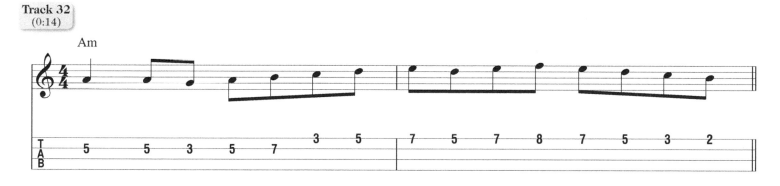

Okay! Here's one last lick, also in A minor, that will bring you back to the root chord after coming off the E7.

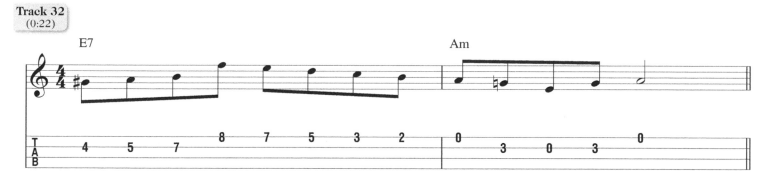

The Flatt Run

The Flatt Run is a famous fill, synonymous with bluegrass legend Lester Flatt (of Flatt & Scruggs fame). This is a highly versatile lick that can be used often.

Track 33
(0:00)

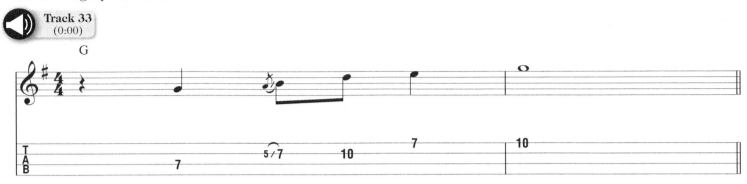

Here is a variation with eighth notes in the key of G.

Track 33
(0:07)

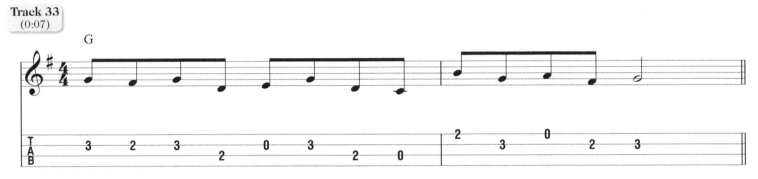

Okay. Now we'll try a Flatt run in C with a little slide.

Track 33
(0:15)

This next one is just like our variation with eighth notes (for all of you low G players), again in C.

Track 33
(0:23)

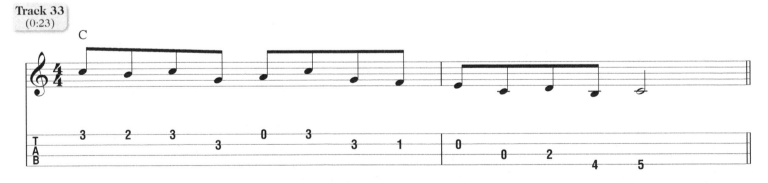

Ear Notes: If you really want to get a good feel for the Flatt run, I recommend listening to the now-classic *Foggy Mountain Jamboree* album, recorded by Lester Flatt and Earl Scruggs in 1957 for Columbia.

Shave-and-a-Haircut Licks

The "Shave-and-a-Haircut" lick came of age during the golden years of the bluegrass revival in the 1960s. It is most synonymous with the Beverly Hillbillies' theme (performed by Flatt & Scruggs). Use this lick with folk, bluegrass, country, or even Tin Pan Alley tunes.

Key of C

Track 34
(0:00)

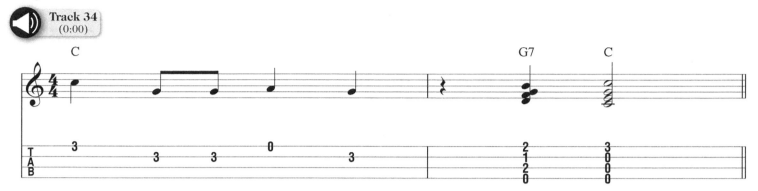

Key of D

Track 34
(0:09)

Key of F

Track 34
(0:17)

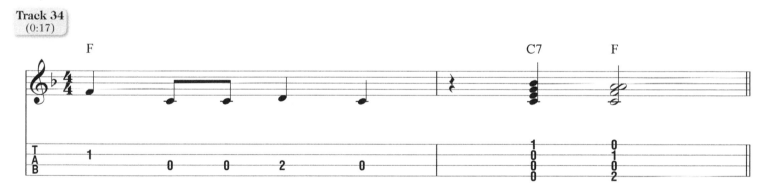

Key of A

Track 34
(0:27)

Bluegrass Chords & Scales

Typical Bluegrass Chord Progression in G

 Track 35

Scales Often Used

- C, D, and G Major Pentatonic
- C, D, and G Minor Pentatonic
- C, D, and G Mixolydian

Recommended Listening	
Artist	**Album/Song Title**
Tony Rice	*Plays and Sings Bluegrass*
The Stanley Brothers	*An Evening Long Ago: Live 1956*
The Charles River Valley Boys	*Beatle Country*
Norman Blake	*Whiskey Before Breakfast*
The Carter Family	*The Millennium Collection*
Del McCoury	*By Request*
Jerry Garcia/David Grisman	*Jerry Garcia/David Grisman*
Lil' Rev	"Dreamers Waltz"
James Hill	"Ode to a Frozen Boot"
Jake Shimabukuro	"Bluegrass Ukulele"
Flatt & Scruggs	*Foggy Mountain Jamboree*

The Third Wave Ukulele Revival

Beginning in 1996 and 1997, the Ukulele Hall of Fame Museum began to sponsor ukulele expos across the eastern seaboard. The expo experience combined performances by the day's top ukulele players alongside workshops, hall of fame induction ceremonies, open mics, vendors, retailers, and historical lectures—all rolled into one fabulous event. As word eventually began to spread, ukulele builders, players, and aspiring amateurs started to arrive on America's shores from all over the world, looking to commune with mainland players, and, in turn, to take that inspiration back across the Atlantic.

As these expos began to attract national attention, a full-throttled ukulele revival ensued. This, in turn, opened the door to a blossoming of grass-roots clubs and ukulele festivals in Los Angeles, CA; Bellingham, WA; Seattle, WA; San Francisco, CA; Indianapolis, IN; New York, NY; Milwaukee, WI; Santa Cruz, CA; Cerritos, CA; Portland, OR; Lake Tahoe, NV; Chicago, IL; Tampa Bay, FL; and other locales. Today there are ukulele clubs and festivals sprouting up faster than any blog, manufacturer, or music store can possibly keep up with!

While the ukulele's popularity has never waned in many parts of the world like Hawaii, various pockets of the Pacific Islands, and Canada, it has enjoyed fleeting periods of boom and bust stateside, first starting in the early teens, followed by a short resurgence of interest in the 1950s with Arthur Godfrey, and later in 1968 with Tiny Tim (and the entire folk revival in the 1960s).

Looking back today at over ten straight years of ukulelemania, it is easy to understand why we are now witnessing an explosion of interest in our humble, little jumping flea. From Bill Macy (on Oprah) to the band Train (on *Dancing with the Stars*), from *American Idol* to commercials and *SpongeBob Squarepants*, it is now cool to be seen and heard playing the uke!

On YouTube, we can thank ukulele god Jake Shimabukuro's jaw-dropping version of "While My Guitar Gently Weeps" for helping to build the momentum with over six million hits.

A huge tip of the hat should also go out to "Jumpin'" Jim Beloff, whose songbooks have helped get us all started. Likewise, his web site, www.fleamarketmusic.com, has provided a networking platform for ukulele players all over the world.

Today's crop of professional ukulele players are pushing the boundaries of what pop culture ever presumed to be possible to play on a little, old, four-string instrument. These players include: Del Rey, Jim Beloff, Brooke Adams, James Hill, Joel Eckhaus, John King, Ralph Shaw, Dr. Byron Yasui, Lyle Ritz, Bill Tapia, Travis Harrelson, Aldrine Guerrero, Craig Chee, Jake Shimabukuro, Aaron Keim, Gerald Ross, Victoria Vox, Brittni Paiva, Troy Fernandez, Azo Bell, Herb Ohta, Herb Ohta, Jr., Daniel Ho, and yours truly… Lil' Rev!

The Ukulele in Rock 'n' Roll

While Tiny Tim was notorious for recording songs like "Stairway to Heaven" and "Hey, Jude," most will agree that Mr. Tim was more of a song collector than a real rocker on the ukulele. With that said, it is undeniable that the ukulele has begun to reach blazing new heights in the hands of Jake Shimabukuro and James Hill (to name two). Just check out Jake's YouTube version of George Harrison's "While My Guitar Gently Weeps," which, at the time of this writing, has been viewed over six million times. As it turns out, George Harrison was a true uke-a-holic, and was not only known to take a ukulele wherever he went, but was also fond of giving them away as gifts.

These days, it's hip and trendy to be seen with a ukulele, and everyone from Pearl Jam's Eddie Vedder to Warren Zevon and Pete Townshend have been known to play the ukulele both in concert and on wax. And if that isn't enough proof that the ukulele is "on the march" (to use Ian Whitcomb's song title), just have a listen to the Ukulele Orchestra of Great Britain playing "Johnny B. Goode" or the Troggs' "Wild Thing," and this should be all the convincing one needs to realize that the third wave ukulele revival is in full swing. And maybe, just maybe, rock 'n' roll isn't dead after all...

The World's Greatest Rock 'n' Roll Lick

Well, maybe this isn't the world's greatest rock 'n' roll lick, but it does highlight many of the main ingredients in a legendary lick: repetition, simplicity, and driving rhythm. Chuck Berry took full advantage of both the major and minor pentatonic scales while leaning heavily on double stops, staccato attacks, and some of the most beautifully simplistic playing that the rock world has ever known. And for this, he will be eternally emulated.

Bonus Licks!

Play this lick repetitively over any changes in A.

Here's a cool Chuck Berry lick to play over the V chord (E), utilizing more double stops.

Instruments & Builders

So often in my travels, folks ask me where they should go to purchase a good ukulele. This list will guide you on your journey through the maze that has become the ukulele marketplace.

Low- to Mid-Range-Priced Instruments

www.kalaukulele.com – Kala offers top-notch customer service and an impressive inventory of starter to mid-ranged-level ukuleles. Made overseas.

www.mainlandukuleles.com – This Indiana-based company picked up where Bushman left off in that their ukuleles are beautiful, solid-wood, hand-crafted instruments that are made in South America (with the final setup at their factory in Indiana). Expect top-quality customer service and expedient delivery from these guys.

www.fleamarketmusic.com – "Jumpin'" Jim Beloff can not only take credit for helping to spearhead the current ukulele revival with his great books and videos, but his company, The Magic Fluke, is one of the only mainland ukulele companies that is cranking out affordable instruments for the beginning ukulele player. These ukuleles are fun to play and look at—and why not support a uke that is made in the USA?

Mid- to High-Range-Priced Instruments

www.koolauukulele.com – The Ko'olau Guitar and Ukulele Company, based in Wahiawa, HI, makes fabulous ukuleles for the seldom-found, mid-range-level player and buyer. If you are looking for a nice mahogany or koa ukulele, look no further than Pono.

www.kamakahawaii.com   Carrying on a tradition of custom-built Hawaiian ukuleles for almost one hundred years, Kamaka is the source for mid-high-quality soprano, pineapple, concert, tenor, 6-, 8-, and 10-string ukuleles. You simply can't go wrong with a Kamaka!

www.ukemaker.com – California-based ukulele builder Michael DaSilva not only has the coolest studio in which to work and host ukulele events, but also builds some of the finest custom instruments on the mainland.

www.myamoeukuleles.com – Another personal favorite of mine, this husband-and-wife team out of White Salmon, Washington, builds exquisite resonator, tenor, baritone, concert, and soprano ukuleles. For the level of quality, these ukuleles can't be beat for value, appearance, or overall playability. I am constantly impressed with the craftsmanship of these fine instruments!

www.grazianoukuleles.com – Tony Graziano has received a lot of great press over the years, and it is all well deserved as this California-based builder has few peers when it comes to both aesthetics and playability. Tony is a consummate craftsman who takes great pride in seeing his instruments in the hands of those who will enjoy ukulele playing for years!

www.charguitars.com – Portland, Oregon's Kerry Char is world renowned for his attention to detail, traditional styling, and meticulous restoration of classic string instruments.

www.thebeansprout.com – Looking for a banjo ukulele? Well, Bean Sprout serves up a hearty dish for those who are looking to play old-time, blues, and jug band music on a banjo ukulele.

Cool Music-Related Web Sites

Navigating the worldwide web can be daunting. With new sites constantly emerging, it is hard to know where to turn for ukulele news, reviews, videos, theory, and more. After years of surfing the web, I have narrowed it down for you. What follows are useful and essential sites for all levels.

www.ukulelian.blogspot.com – This is one of my favorite blogs for general info, new releases, great videos, and the ukulele in world news.

www.fleamarketmusic.com – Nobody has done more to uplift the humble ukulele in this modern era than Jim Beloff. From his cool Fluke Ukuleles to his numerous songbooks, Jim's site is a valuable resource not only because of his online store and jukebox, but because of his concise ukulele club listing, chat room, and bulletin board.

www.ezfolk.com – This is a site that every player should know about. It has tons of tabs, chords/songs, books, instruments, and so much more.

www.elderly.com – Elderly Instruments is one of the single greatest online mail order stores for music-related merchandise in the country. When in Lansing, MI, visit their store as well.

digital.library.ucla.edu/sheetmusic/ – If you are into old music, this is a great resource for old sheet music— pre-1922 public domain material posted by the UCLA-at-Davis.

www.oldtimeherald.org – This is the single greatest magazine strictly dedicated to old time music.

www.singout.org – Magazine that preserves and supports cultural diversity and heritage through music, writings, and events.

www.ukuleleguild.org/index.php – A guild dedicated to the preservation, perpetuation, and continuation of all things ukulele worldwide.

www.oldtownschool.org – One of a small handful of historic music organizations in the country dedicated to perpetuating the folk arts through lessons, concerts, and workshops. A must visit when in Chicago.

www.pdinfo.com – Avoid copyright infringement by knowing both the laws and the tunes available for us all to use. Anything composed prior to 1922 is fair game. Because the ukulele world relies heavily on old time favorites, this site is a must for every ukulele player. Public domain song listing.

www.folkways.si.edu – The literal treasure trove of American roots music still available to the public. Discover the most important online sound catalog in the world.

www.halleonard.com – The world's largest music print publisher!

Ukulele Festivals

Here is a list of my favorite mainland ukulele festivals and camps. If you are a true uke-a-holic, you will find your way to one of these inspirational celebrations of all things uke! A good ukulele festival should boast at least one day of workshops, vendors, concerts, and jamming.

Colorado Ukulele Festival

www.swallowhillmusic.org/festivals/UkeFest2010 – This lovely, little ukulele festival is sponsored by the Swallow Hill Music Organization, and holds court in early February. Expect an eclectic array of performers and styles.

The Eugene Uke-Tober Fest

www.uketoberfest.com – This fine festival is the brainchild of uke master Brooke Adams. It is held every October in Eugene, OR.

Gorge Ukulele Festival

www.gorgeukuleles.org – In the beautiful Columbia River Gorge in Hood River, OR, this is one of the best-kept secrets in the ukulele world—small, charming, and full of awesome surprises every year. Sponsored by the good folks at Mya-Moe Ukuleles and held in February/March, this festival is highly recommended.

Lone Star Ukulele Festival

www.lonestarukefest.com – Visit the great state of Texas for a big bang of a good time. Expect Hawaiian, Texas swing, blues, jazz, and much more! This is annually held in April/May.

Milwaukee Ukulele Festival

www.mufest.com – Come for beer and cheese, but stay for the grandest little ukulele festival in the Midwest! This annual festival attracts fans from all over the world who come for one full day of workshops, concerts, vendors, and jamming—plus the coolest post-uke-fest late-night party!

New York Ukulele Festival

www.nyukefest.com – What could be better than hanging out in Manhattan for a weekend? This is where you'll hear all the hottest licks! This festival is annually held in May.

Portland Ukulele Festival

www.portlandukefest.org – Hands down, the P.U.F. is the best ukulele training camp in the world. Boasting an impressive roster of well over a dozen instructors, this festival is four days of sheer ukulele madness on the lush campus of Reed College in Portland, OR. This biannual gathering is usually held in the early summer months.

Wine Country Ukulele Festival

www.winecountryukefest.com – California is king when it comes to ukulele clubs and festivals. From the Hayward Festival to Cerritos, California is the place to be! The annual September Wine Country festival is quickly becoming California's premier ukulele festival.

Recommended Listening

The following ukulele recordings are among my personal favorites. This list represents a great number of players and styles; some of these legends have passed on, but most are still with us. This is but a very small piece of the pie!

Azo Bell - *Alibi of Birdland* (2002)
(Azo Bell is a consummate instrumentalist, brimming with tasteful licks. He is utterly creative in his approach to playing the ukulele.)

Cliff "Ukulele Ike" Edwards – *Singing in the Rain* (1995)

Brian Hefferan – *Music Box Rag* (2003)
(This guy finds the coolest old tunes—fingerpicked ragtime on a ukulele!)

James Hill – *A Flying Leap* (2005) (Killer chops and mindboggling speed)
James Hill & Anne Davison – *True Love, Don't Weep* (2009)

Israel "Iz" Kamikawiwo'ole – *Tropical Music* (1990)
Israel "Iz" Kamikawiwo'ole – *Facing Future* (1993)

Casey MacGill's Blue 4 Trio – *Three Cool Cats* (2008)
(Swingin' jump, jazz, and jive)

Herb Ohta, Jr. – *Ukulele Romantic* (2003)

Brittni Paiva – *Brittini X3* (2004)
Brittni Paiva – *Four Strings/The Fire Within* (2009)

Del Rey/The Yes Yes Boys – *Why Say No?* (2003)
(Fingerstyle blues on uke)

Lyle Ritz – *How About Uke* (1957 Reissue) (Tons of hot licks on this one)
Lyle Ritz/Herb Ohta – *A Night of Ukulele Jazz – Live at McCabe's* (2001)

Gerald Ross – *Ukulele Stomp* (2005) (Great all-around player)
Gerald Ross – *Ukulele Hit Parade* (2009)

Ohta-San – *Plays the Beatles* (2002)
Ohta-San – *Ukulele Virtuoso/Misty* (2005)

Jake Shimabukuro – *Sunday Morning* (2002) (Blazing skills and hot licks galore!)
Jake Shimabukuro – *Crosscurrents* (2003)

Roy Smeck – *Plays Hawaiian Guitar, Banjo, Ukulele, and Guitar 1926-1949* (1992)

Bill Tapia – *Tropical Swing* (2004) (My all-time, favorite ukulele player!)
Bill Tapia – *Duke of Uke* (2005) (Understated, tasteful jazz soloing)